The Arrow of Time

THE
Arrow
of Time

Bruce Meyer

RONSDALE

THE ARROW OF TIME
Copyright © 2015 Bruce Meyer

RONSDALE PRESS
3350 West 21st Avenue
Vancouver, B.C., Canada V6S 1G7
www.ronsdalepress.com

Typesetting: Julie Cochrane, in New Baskerville 11 pt on 13.5
Cover Design: Julie Cochrane
Paper: Enviro 100 Edition, 55 lb. Antique Cream (FSC) — 100%
    post-consumer waste, totally chlorine-free and acid-free

Ronsdale Press wishes to thank the following for their support of its publishing
program: the Canada Council for the Arts, the Government of Canada through
the Canada Book Fund, the British Columbia Arts Council, and the Province
of British Columbia through the Book Publishing Tax Credit Program.

Library and Archives Canada Cataloguing in Publication

Meyer, Bruce, 1957–, author
  The arrow of time / Bruce Meyer.

Poems.
Issued in print and electronic formats.
ISBN 978-1-55380-428-4 (print)
ISBN 978-1-55380-429-1 (ebook) / ISBN 978-1-55380-430-7 (pdf)

  I. Title.

PS8576.E93A87 2015   C811'.54   C2015-902992-9   C2015-902993-7

At Ronsdale Press we are committed to protecting the environment. To this
end we are working with Canopy (formerly Markets Initiative) and printers to
phase out our use of paper produced from ancient forests. This book is one
step towards that goal.

Printed in Canada by Marquis Book Printing, Quebec, Canada

for Kerry, Katie,
Margaret and Carolyn

"Let us draw an arrow arbitrarily. If as we follow the arrow we find more and more random elements in the state of the world, then the arrow is pointing to the future; if the random element decreases, the arrow points toward the past . . . the introduction of randomness is the only thing which cannot be undone."

— ARTHUR EDDINGTON,
The Nature of the Physical World (1928)

"I believe things cannot make themselves impossible."

— STEPHEN HAWKING

CONTENTS

– Expansion –

– Increase –

– Entropy –

– Expansion –

Young Rembrandt, 1637

Before snow settles on the roof
and even a mere thought of winter
is something other people think,

there is that time when the chin
in a portrait is lifted up,
when seriousness in the eyes

is read as thoughtful ambition,
a time to take on the world,
to know time can be replaced,

the first easel, the first chair,
and a table where works poured
as if melt water from a glacier,

fresh but untouched in its path.
He is wearing a painter's cap,
as black as the one he recalls

years later when patrons
posed like water in a rain storm
on a mild December afternoon.

It is late in the day. The sun
wants to lock up and go home —
but in this instance the eyes

are bright enough to read by
and they look into time
to say spring waits just ahead

in a place he believes is April.
Look into the future with him.
Does he see the way ahead?

Such an image is a captive.
The future finds it all familiar;
yet the heart knows what it loves —

even so, it is better to remember
what was than to forget,
the taste of good, surprising wine

as beautiful as the first sip
at the world's last supper
to quench love's long test of life.

Seven Magpies

When I lived in England
and my train stopped at country stations
there was always the feeling
that someone beneath a farm field
was staring back at me —

someone buried and forgotten,
a village no longer extant,
house and church and graveyard
cobbler and carter, their wives and children
and children's children
all memory palimpsest
as apples fallen where the tree stood

and if I disembarked and walked out
in wellies through the brown-black earth
I might be sucked under by history.

I don't have that feeling when a train
stops at Bradford platform
and the car fills with the pungent smell
of green onions picked and ploughed under
with the aroma of work and sweat still vital
after a season in the Ontario sun;

that if I put my ear to the ground
no one is calling out in agony
as their flesh fails beneath the plague
and the autumn wind consumes them
with hunger and hoarfrost and namelessness

for among the deep tangle of weed roots
and the worm eager to please as best he can
all I hear is the silence of former trees
gently giving up their leaves to autumn light
and waiting for someone to remember they were here.

Masterpieces

As Wilson Bentley photographed flakes
in the barn of his Vermont farm, he knew
that each unique creation passing before
his eyes into the timelessness of forever
was a small masterpiece that never again
would grace the world as individual.

Today in the gallery, in each individual
frame, I peered into small worlds. Flakes
of art lovers' dust settled again and again
on the varnished surfaces, and I knew
that man is as much the enemy of forever
as time, and our best efforts stand before

us as reminders of our brief lives. Before
man learned to paint, he had the individual
stars, the stories they told set forever
against the unknown; in the cold, the flakes
fell from heaven because heaven knew
that even it was beyond permanence. Again,

I watch snowstorms, updrafts rising again
and falling until the dance is madness before
the emptiness of death. Wilson Bentley believed
that the universe was ruled by an individual
mind constantly seeking a singular snowflake,
the brevity that is beauty. Nothing lasts forever.

Art and snowstorms are reminders that forever
is a rare moment when nothing dies, yet again,
nature mistakes originality for effort; snowflakes,
each unique, must be crafted in time before
time's end. The storms will exhaust individual
possibilities to prove there are limits we knew

to exist, but have never proven. If we knew
the end of things, we might stop trying, and forever
lose that vision that makes us individual,
that *maniera* so frail yet so strong we gain
purpose, testing our minds before
our time ends. We are kin to snowflakes,

and if we knew we were a beauty that never again
will exist, we would struggle to last forever before
we melt, leaving a tear as individual as a snowflake.

The Anatomy of Tea

for Ida Evelyn Reid Miller, 1893–1975

The bottom of every china cup
held the magic of the future
and the sadness of the past.
As if looking into a pool

for a reflection of the moon,
or the night sky for strength,
Ida conjured a rainy hillside
of a northern Indian mountain

as a phrase she could taste,
bitter on the tip of her tongue.
It was prophecy. Sad memories
of a fallen empire, the sun

setting through a kitchen window,
the room darker by the minute
as if leaves set to steep
the length of the Lord's Prayer —

and wherever the prayer brewed
the word spread for good or bad
until a map bled bright red
into a cup of hibiscus zinger.

I came home exhausted tonight.
It is still winter, and flowers
are fragments of ancient history.
An emperor's jasmine bloomed

with the scent of a spring garden
filled with a perfume of divine April,
and it rose from the twisting vapours
where a dancer with brass cymbals

rang the clear bright notes
to revive that haunting instinct
to stand between time and eternity
where the view of terraced slopes

and the thought of rain vanishing
over celadon-coloured mountains
left me feeling I could breathe again.
I could see so clearly in the twilight

to the bottom of the warm cup,
and I grasped in my cold hands
the sparkling serenity after rain
of Buddha beneath the banyan tree.

Crystal Set

On summer nights I would drop a wire
from the sill of my bedroom window
and with a headset
split like a wishbone
sing along to a night of stars —

Elvis Presley, Perry Como —
each broken-hearted troubadour
telling me to fall in love;

for even powerless tunes were magic,
and all the melodies that filled my head
from an earphone tucked beneath my pillow
could not answer the questions of life
that outlived the music
inside my mind.

I want to remember how I listened,
but to amplify such innocence,
the passing charms and distant signals
received through the ash tree of my backyard,
would ask the heart to listen harder
and betray the litany of a popular song;

so I remain faithful to what is powerless
to hear the evidence of things not seen,
and catch the music of a wishing-star
as fragile as a crystal sphere
when it crackles from the end of time.

Elegy for the Bees

If you saw a violet open
with snow on purple petals,

or a rose announce itself
with the perfume of an uncorrupted saint,

or white become more white
than snow on an April day

when the bees should have returned
to proclaim the beginning of spring,

then you would know
why honey is sweeter than love,

and why dawn breaking is a phrase
for dew upon weeping fields.

Persian Apples

To the flat medieval palate,
the east was a place of spice
and sweetness all flowing

through the holy shrines of Jerusalem.
A diet of salt turnips and meat
aged until it spoke to itself

was a far cry from the gates of heaven.
Imagine when a knight passing
through the mysteries of Byzantium

first tasted a peach, the juices
on his tongue as if a sacrament,
the stone clinging fast to its flesh

the way a zealot clings to faith.
He could picture in every bite
the Hanging Gardens of Babylon,

and the taste of every temporal delight.
He had no way of knowing how far
away the Persian apple tasted,

how a court scribe sitting in the shade
of an emperor's red pagoda bit
into an identical fruit and knew

the dragon splendour of perfection.
A leaf falls from a draped willow,
and ripples bring the koi to feast,

their peach-gold bodies shimmering.
Each early August at the height
of an Ontario summer, the perfume

of sweet freestones fills my kitchen,
and the down of red and gold
gives up its stony heart

until there is nothing left but beauty.
I tell you this now because the world,
as it ripens, is delicate as a peach.

Explaining Romanticism
to My Daughter

It is always like snow falling in the heart,
and we both turn to stare out the window.

Flakes descend as softly as moonlight,
but in the time it takes to watch the trees,

to catch the broken sky in empty hands,
the wind howls around the house and cries

with the pain and pity of a grieving silence
where the world must be rebuilt for life.

It is the difference between the way snow fell
and what it could tell you of its fall from heaven.

Complications

This is a complicated world.
Everything moves because it must.
The moon, the stars, the sun —
all are measured complications.

The date and time are easy.
They are only apparent complications,
but when the snow is falling,
when the night is thick with clouds,

that's when complications begin.
There are stars behind the clouds.
They are constant, but complicated.
How do the stars really work?

You cannot strap science to your wrist
and think you know everything;
but when the first ray of light
tries to lift its shattered body

over the park across the street
to show you how it snowed last night,
and the exhaustion in every bone
makes you feel each tiny movement,

remember how chimes sound, the voice
of time calling through the house
as you lie awake beside me in the dark.
It is complicated, but here we are.

Strawberries

i

My daughter is a strawberry blond
with a high forehead and grey eyes.

She reminds me of those delicate women
seated in the margins of medieval books,

their lark-like fingers holding a heart
as if a locket from a departed love

who gave his beauty by dying for life.
The day is hung with a veil of breath,

and strawberries are the earth's reminders
how the world learned to breathe again,

waking to every dream-vision April
as apple trees burst to blossom

the way the pages of a book of hours
open timelessly to tell the time.

Footsteps in a heavenly garden
tread softly not to wake the rose,

and found instead the perfect berry,
so full of love it had to be love.

ii

Red is for sacrifice, the monks pronounced:
the colour of pain, sweetness, and prayer,

a ruby heart with its gospel of seeds,
tiny St. Christophers that grow inside you,

the future of faith in a world beyond winter.
The European bauble and Virginian fruit

evolved today's common garden *fragaria,*
the perfume of saints and the taste of bread.

It is easy to confuse such beauty with faith;
the Romans thought strawberries healed,

their sweetness inspired troubadour song,
and the taste demanded hymns of praise;

for what vanishes in our mouths like prayers
is why lovers placed them on each other's tongues

as larks and bluebirds chant the meadows
and the fields hold baskets of sweet love.

iii

I tasted my first strawberry at a church social.
The women wore big hats and had loud voices,

and the laughing roses of their flowered dresses
shamed the heavy heads of white hydrangea

as clouds billowed and tumbled with light,
and puffed with dollops of whipped cream.

Understand nature knows both horror and love,
and sent us strawberries to taste of rainbows,

and reassure us our celebrations are good.
Some of the men recalled opening jam tins

with the business ends of their bayonets,
and when dark clouds burst above their heads

everyone ran for cover except one man
who merely smoothed his white moustache

as the gentle blessing of the sky's bombardment
fell upon him and darkened his soul.

He simply sat there with his paper plate,
the strawberries floating in a sea of red.

iv

The truth of strawberries is that nature made one
and men took charge and made the others;

found Virginian forests had many hearts
and married their fragrance to chivalric tastes.

The French discovered desire could be grown,
and seeded their plants in long, tufted rows

so desire would mark the beginning of summer,
and lovers would exchange their hearts

dipped in sugar or on angel-food cakes.
But love must always consume itself,

must vanish like fireflies to conquer all,
and each time two lovers lie back and sigh

there is always that sweetness they remember,
the sweetness of summer, of touch and taste.

Just before dawn I saw an angel in our garden,
his hands feathering through the strawberry patch,

and I told him to eat as many as he wanted;
he replied heaven would taste of this fruit.

– Increase –

Turner's Spectacles

By staring at the sun for years
a man learns truth in blindness,
wears thick spectacles to see
just how far an eye might reach,
the presbyopic beauty of stars,
the blurred image of things close.
Ruskin understood Turner's light.

When Turner died, Ruskin found
eyewear for the far-sighted mind,
for ascertaining how a painter's knife
might cut a blended landscape
into clouds, or blended clouds
into angels both bright and dark.
In "Rain, Speed, and Steam," a train

emerges from the hand of nature,
its dark spectre harrowing the sky,
the smoke choking a path through light,
and its trestle marring infinite green.
Turner knew the struggles of time,
knew that in seeing he saw fate
as it haunts a conscience to death;

and his death mask is a face agape,
his mind open with one last gasp
to swallow the living light like water
and quench the lips of a thirsting world.
On closer inspection the details speak:
not the gurgling of a body drained,
but the music of a rising sun, whispers

of a day unnamed. Energy, said Blake,
is pure delight, and despite the pain,
the frailty of the human accident,
life shines if only by mere candle,
and the road to Babylon is paved in stars
so one learns how they can be read,
and put to words the secrets they keep.

Thirst

When Richard the Lionheart
laid siege to Jerusalem,
he begged the Emperor Saladin

to slake his thirst in the heat.
The emperor sent him fruit
and snow from the holy city

to remind him of unquenchable quests,
just as today when Garcia Marquez
lay dying in Mexico City

he dreamt of his father
and the day in the mountains
he caught his first glimpse of snow.

For if I try to tell a story
and my tongue thirsts
to speak of rain or snow

I know this story has to end
with no way of understanding
how the firmament can be replenished,

or how drops, or flakes in their descent,
are birds that tried to fly too high
and fell to earth as legends

when no one was there to listen.

Marigolds

The boy retches at the acrid smell
of his grandfather's hands. The blood
of marigolds stains his pappy's fingers
to dark green, the beautiful green
of songbirds and young apples growing
on the boughs of an old delicious.

The boy thinks flowers are delicious,
a fragrance of roses bursting to the smell
of uncorrupted saints, a growing
wonder that a spirit in gardens and blood
was the way love made things green:
souls of men, prayers held in fingers,

blossoms awakened by touch. His fingers
were brown, but held that delicious
musk of earthworms and small green
weeds, lives touched by light, the smell
of life reaching for heaven, the sun's blood
making things grow and keep growing.

Then time happened. As a boy growing
up in North Toronto, he kept his fingers
crossed that all the life in a garden's blood
would bless him with that delicious
love saints possess, a love they smell
in roses, the scent of grace, the green

in flowers that blackens the way green
leaves glow orange then fall, growing
into soil and feeding marigolds the smell
of lilies, while the scent of peonies in fingers
of undertakers masked death with delicious
aromas of eternity. He watched. His blood

lost the flower of stories as the blood
drained from his grandfather into the green
sluices of memory. The apples were delicious,
but now were windfalls; the garden growing
by itself went to seed. The sun's fingers
took back the light, and a black smell

haunted the boy, the delicious sun growing
dim with winter. The flowers' green blood
clutched his fingers with the smell of marigolds.

Adam and Eve

after Lucas Cranach
ut animata viderent Dominum natum

The ventured guess is love's foundation.
Mere curiosity. Delight in the unknown.
In Cranach's painting, Adam is thinking.
He scratches his head, weighs the cause
and effect. Eve, already full of knowledge
the way a beloved sees the road ahead,
is smiling. She is certain. The taste,
not unlike communion wine, is sweet.
She has seen the future. Her yellow apple
is the best from the tree. The animals,
however, show concern: the horned stag
is on the verge of weeping but cannot.
A pair of partridges peck the ground,
enjoying one last carefree meal. The lion
crouches knowing what is to come,
and the boar's tusks are suddenly revealed
to show the world the meaning of power.
Love is knowledge; these two begin
a curriculum with tests of shadows,
questions of love, pain, beauty and desire
as long as they shall share the fruit,
waking beside each other every morning,
feeling the cold of their room as life
around them warms to the necessity
of a day spent making more days ahead
until they exhaust the fabric of time.
But it is the doe to the lower right
that speaks to what one gives for love:
with one last look, she sees herself
framed in a pool as pure as sunrise.

Never again will she be this beautiful.
She will wear her nervous trembling
and remember how the great white horse
emerged at that moment, as if by miracle,
to study a bad decision yet survive it,
aware that love, the greatest truth of all,
endures beyond the garden and the tree.
Every creature, every living thing
will remember this moment as the day
love and death became masters of life
with one more powerful than the other —
one the answer, the other the question —
as death answered, life became mystery,
and the need to know became the need to love.

Jigsaw

So, we shall take a moment
    to put the moment together,
a second to make the first thing
    into everything that is right,
and the time to be the ones
    who hold time in abeyance;
for there is always love in a passing moment
    except what passes for love in the moment,
and know what is true is what we feel,
    and what we feel is the truth inside,
so we must take a moment
    to put the moment together.

Have you seen the puzzle's picture?
    Have you counted all the pieces?
Have you laid the jigsaw on the table
    and realized it has one piece more?
The clock is on us, the minute passes,
    can we embrace what's next
for most of the time is spent in giving
    and the rest in giving more,
so take a moment to put it all together —
    show me the picture. Make it all complete.

The Arrow of Time

Driving by houses after dark,
I can see into the lives of others

the way a shoe-laced family album
leaves me embarrassed to eavesdrop

on a time through dated, decaled frames.
Everything leaves a shadow behind:

a woman holding my infant mother,
a box sedan that carried relatives

to places where their lives took place
and cannot happen again; the trail

through trees that arch and meet
the way grandparents held hands —

all fixed in neat triangular corners
on a page as starless as memory.

Do you think they look back at us,
those ancestors stored in a cool dark place,

and through portals in time's safety fence
watch our faint, illumined hour develop,

growing dimmer as we vector forward,
until the lamps in living room windows

are extinguished like possibilities
and the time we made fades to black?

Hans Memling's "The Donne Triptych"

The donors could be cleaned up.
Flattery comes in brushstrokes.
To find the perfect Virgin face,

he would have to look beyond
the crowded streets of Bruges,
past the river where the plague dead

were washed out to sea on tears
of angels and April rains, past
the crumbling footprints left

by time, winter, and market stalls.
He would have to find the face
of heaven, the face of love,

in a world that afforded little.
Her forehead would be broad,
her fair hair flowing like a prayer,

and her downcast eye caring
with love for the scrambling infant
seated on her lap. He gave her

a book, and although the girl
he found could not read a word,
he knew she felt the child's great weight

pressing on her thighs. An angel
holds a tiny orb. The child reaches
for it as if the world is a toy,

while a second angel on the left
bears an instrument of soft harmony,
imagining heaven full of music

to wake the world to life again.
In the distance, a mill wheel turns,
catching handfuls of a passing stream,

to describe to nature how time passes,
embracing seasons and denying them,
while a peacock, perched atop a wall,

awaits the moment when life is sown
and the miller, always hungry for its love,
holds a sack for the grim harvest.

There is a figure standing on a bridge
far in the distance, almost beyond reach,
perhaps as far as the heart can dream,

and he bears the burden of his soul
the way one carries a story through life,
for he is the voice who recounts all this;

and the Virgin's eyes are closed to see
what only the face of heaven observes,
and the pages of her book foretell it all.

All stories end with time, though most
exhaust the teller and the mortal voice,
the way a winter night is but a tale,

and the child, hand upon a crumpled page,
declares the end will be his to write,
cum Sancto Spiritu, in gloria Dei Patris.

The Preliminary

We see nothing truly until we understand it.

— John Constable

i

The way one sees something at first,
the way Constable sketched his home,
is where passion marries beauty to thirst.

The Stour at East Bergholt is the purest
expression of the imagination, a welcome
the way one sees something at first

and that glance of the eye, that tourist
perception of a new world to come,
is where passion marries beauty to thirst.

The house, the willow heavy, the surest
green of bank-side reeds, a meadow, all sum
the way one sees something at first.

What one loves and loves well is the clearest
benchmark in a life of blank canvases from
where passion marries beauty to thirst

and the preliminary vision appears to burst
its frame and shatter artistic decorum;
for the way one sees something at first
is how passion marries beauty to thirst.

ii

Look at the river; see how the cloudy sky
makes what is familiar into polished silver,
reflecting not only the heart but heaven's eye.

If a painting is a window to the soul, try
to imagine the brush as the hand of a painter.
Look at the river. See how the cloudy sky

appears to move over the willows by
the riverbank, the reeds ready to shimmer
and reflect not only the heart but heaven's eye.

Constable's *East Bergholt* exemplifies why
an artist must know what he can identify.
Look at the river and see how a cloudy sky

is both time and timeless, that deft reality
one frames as if a window on life where
one can reflect on the heart and heaven's eye

and how lifeless art can never die.
Here is a sketch of faith to last forever,
and look at the river, the cloudy sky,
and all it reflects. The artist is heaven's eye.

iii

If there is wind in the sky, this preliminary
canvas for a much larger work might hold,
in a single breath expressing his philosophy,

a spirit that lives in a brushstroke; every
nuance announces itself. Time can unfold
if there is wind in the sky, as in this preliminary

canvas; the white inn against the verdancy
of his birthplace declares that he beholds
in a single breath expressing his philosophy

the life he wants us to know, a complicity
between artist and subject that explodes
like wind in a heavy sky. These preliminary

observations are not criticism, but a joy
that infuses the spirit, a virtue that extols,
in a single breath, expressing his philosophy,

the beauty of being alive in a world as lovely
as what is born into it, with questions as bold
as a south wind caught in a rough preliminary,
where a single breath inspires his philosophy.

    iv

And there he was in the moment,
alive and aware that all around him
nature was a gift heaven sent,

where a flock of birds on the current
of wind illustrates a moment's rhythm;
and there he was in the moment

standing back from it all, observant,
even hesitant, in love with the problem
that nature was a puzzle heaven sent.

To see it now, *The White Horse*, the pent-
up sky pushing at the shores of the frame —
and there he is in the moment —

is to draw a breath of pure discernment
of the kind Wordsworth declared in a hymn
to nature, praising the gift that heaven sent,

yet seeking liberty in it from the indulgence
of art's rules, the past, and the past's form
that keeps him from that fleeting moment
of freedom, the gift that is heaven sent.

v

You are part of this landscape, he says
as he puts his brush down and watches
the changing light remain constant for all days.

The White Horse, East Bergholt, stays
in the mind the way something rare catches
you in a landscape of thought and says

that beyond sentiment or memories
of how things change, a shard of life teaches
us to love the light that remains for all our days,

so that the eye can entertain forever in ways
that give back more life in small snatches
than just being part of a landscape. It says

for all the raw power of nature that plays
upon field, and river, and wild river thatches,
an artist's light remains constant. Life's days

are short. Death is unframed. See how it toys
with you; but art lets you stand back. It watches
you as you move in this landscape. Time says
light dies, but no. It is with you all your days.

vi

Examine the birds in that instant
they are held aloft forever, the sudden
statements in brushwork of a love well spent.

Kenneth Clarke saw the soul of a moment
in the way their wings spread wide when
the artist and the birds in that instant

become one heart and mind, a spirit bent
on discovering new heights through open
statements of colour, a love well spent.

Look — there in the clouds: what he meant
to show was death and rebirth and then
examine how the birds in that instant

are transformed into ideas, energy pent-
up and waiting to take wing, to begin
their freedom in brushwork of a love well spent.

Whatever inspired the world meant
us to see a rainbow breaking over Salisbury plain.
Examine the birds of Constable's moment.
They are the brushwork of a love well spent.

vii

How is it we see life in static art
yet take for granted a morning in July
when every growing thing declares its part

in the chorus of life and death? Apart
from being an English landscape, do you see
how it is that such life in static art

embraces the sound of a cuckoo, the upstart
lapping sounds of the Stour, the sky
echoing every living thing, declaring its part

in the spirit that awakens to report
the art of nature, and the reasons why
we see life as more than static art?

Listen carefully. The white horse pulling a cart
along the broken cinder path can justify
every growing thing that declares its part

as it stops to eat tufts of grass. And to start
the whole machine of water, earth, and sky,
there must have been an artist whose static art
sprang to life, inspired to proclaim his part.

viii

Familiarity is the mother of creativity,
but only a fine eye can see and know
the hardest thing to imagine is familiarity.

Constable knew each reed and willow tree
musing over its reflection to self-bestow
familiarity. Is the mother of creativity

always present? With reservation, he would say
yes, because that is the way we know
the hardest answers. To imagine familiarity,

to share the beauty of it all with clarity
and grace, is what draws one so close to
the familiar, that the mother of creativity

devoured by time leaves only a canvas to see
the truth that is the soul of nature, the flow
of one image into another, the familiarity

that voiceless things must use, the ubiquity
of the commonplace celebrated to show
familiarity as the mother of creativity
where nothing remains except its familiarity.

ix

His home in East Bergholt was torn down
during his lifetime, and Constable died young.
The inn remains, but in the small oil it is shown

as a white thatched building, now painted brown
and lost in the fields. Nothing lasts long.
His home in East Bergholt was torn down.

The Stour is lower now, and through town
it has been diverted to run among
his home's remains; but in the small oil it is shown

as a bridged stream, a river one can own
in one's dreams or memories that belong
to his home in East Bergholt. Tear down

any ideas of meeting Constable. He is gone,
and with him the places in frames that throng
the gallery walls. In a small canvas shown

at a retrospective, his life's work thrown
haphazard in time, the puzzle assembled just long
enough to see East Bergholt, the rolling downs,
river musk, lark songs: all that cannot be not shown.

X

Set on something greater, his sketch finished,
he imagines a canvas of considerable size
but knows in life it will be diminished.

Bacon said God is in small things that vanished
when a person looked away with eyes
set on something greater. His sketch finished,

Constable wanted to say more than perished
ambitions might express with the scene's reprise.
He knew the life in it would be diminished

if it was larger than life; the soul is extinguished
when perceptions become too real to realize.
Set on something greater, his sketch finished,

he lays it in the window of his old room, and rushed
by the need to be elsewhere, life takes him by surprise
and ends too soon. The life in him is not diminished

by the hands of time that have always pushed
the artist until the artist breaks and dies,
but set on something greater, his work unfinished,
the small preliminary canvas lives, undiminished.

The Mathematics of Sunflowers

Everything adds up on a summer evening.
The horizontal light northwest
shines in the heads of sunflowers,
pierces each petal until all eyes are illumined
the way saints' heads are haloed by aureole caps
and every blossom in bright stained glass
is a question of holiness when light fills the world.

Place your hand beneath a drooping head.
It will look up at you as if you brought it mercy,
will show you its Fibonacci face,
the sequence, and order, and life in all things —
for everything adds up on a summer evening

as sunflowers cannot blink at the sun
and desire to voice their maker's plan
to shine in that moment of diurnal grace
with as little self-regard as sunflowers have
for a world they love and a love they die for.

Close your eyes and their image remains.
You are the keeper of a light inside,
and the light in their petals is the voice of prayer;
you must see its secret written on your face,
the way a child holds a cowslip below your chin
and tells you that you must like butter,
or a sunrise refuses to die
until it meets itself in the earth again,
and writes the equation worked by life,
for sunflowers are wisdom's priests.

And if everything adds up on a summer evening,
and small green arms on slender bodies
try to touch you as you move among them,
do you know the innocence alive in them all,
the solitude of stars in a galaxy field,
the space between each reaching leaf,
arms spread wide in their need to hold you?
They are the faces of children who have long grown up.

The Earth was made for fields and sunflowers;
for the sky is blue beyond round flower heads,
and the sun is a sphere to mirror their image;
for everything adds up on a summer evening,
so we stare at the heaven in each other's eyes,
and know all answers are made of light.

– Cause –

Nanking

The bombing of Nanking was never
discussed over Sunday dinner.
Even the sound of a child crying
in another house would pull a curtain
of silence around a conversation,
for what is never said is history.

Most days are forgotten history.
We talk in pleasantries but never
about the past. Polite conversation.
Eat your vegetables. Focus on dinner.
In sunlight through a parlour curtain,
the sound of an ambulance is crying

because it has to be somewhere while crying
for the pain it must visit. That's history,
the small things, things that curtain
off the diffident world, buildings that never
stop burning, the memory of a dinner
interrupted by bombers, conversation

cut short, a wall collapsing, a conversation
with death, a dialogue of endless crying
no heart can stand. For Sunday dinner
we ate silence every anniversary. History
muzzles life. And never, never, never
mention that place: heads rolling in a curtain

of blood while the truth behind the curtain
the world pulled across such conversation
was the truth of Nanking. What is true is never
certain, and what is certain, the bombs crying
as they fell, the pagoda toppled, history
woven from murder . . . ruin a good dinner —

even the thought of it sours a good dinner.
One Hundred Boys dance on the parlour curtain
and look: they appear happy. Their history
saved from a burning mission is a conversation
piece. They are smiling. But wait: one is crying.
Now another. Don't cry. You mustn't. Never.

If you want history, have a conversation
over Sunday dinner with the boy in the curtain.
He is still crying, and he never talks now.

The Thin Man

For a lark, they mounted a camera
on the dashboard of their father's Hudson
and drove around the town before
the city was old enough to realize
how it occupied space on a map,

cut off from the world and on its own,
an inland sea and smelling of axles
and the exhaustion of tired men.
The car turns from the main street
onto a residential side road and stops

in the shade of a flowering chestnut.
Petals are falling on the windshield.
My grandmother and aunt come out
to greet them with smiling poses,
while all around in the uncoloured movie

the world longs to move faster
than the shutter of a wind-up memory.
My father is a young man, younger
than I remember being myself when
I was old enough to swagger and wink.

My aunt stands among her grey roses.
Because it is always spring there,
the petals have not opened and dropped,
and what is being born is still intact
and what has yet to be born remains

untouched, not because time wants
it but because beyond time
there is something far more precious
that has yet to be discovered — maybe
the magic of a moment before moments

that pass before the eyes. My father looks
into the camera, his pencil-thin moustache
is enviable. He has yet to learn to live
and learn to die, and as the lamp goes dark,
he dons a broad fedora and escapes from life.

The Book of Things

Perhaps the poets of the twentieth century are busy
making a catalogue of all existing things.

— Czesław Milosz

I am writing to apologize humbly
to that one beautiful creature
who will be omitted by accident
from the marvellous *Book of Things.*

Its name should have been there,
been set down to outlast time,
honoured, counted, and described.
What isn't there is a terrible loss.

To be named is to be part of life,
to be part of dreams and poetry,
to be loved and remembered well
in the catalogue of all existing things.

What doesn't want to be loved forever,
remembered in both life and death?
Accidents happen. No one is perfect.
So it isn't there in the *Book of Things.*

Death is not as absolute as knowledge.
Death says something has been lost;
but knowledge speaks of a place in life,
legs to move on, thirst at a water hole,

eyes wide awake on a starry night,
the sound of eternity alive in its ears,
a blood, a passion, a need to survive.
It ran away when it was frightened,

mated when the spring rains came,
left a feather engraved in clay,
and was here, and real, and now forgotten.
Say its name and no one will hear.

Perhaps there never was a thing
whose beauty is now mere conjecture.
The great poets will sing its praises
and then be denounced as fools.

Pieta

Look closely at these lines.
You will not find suffering here,
or the pain someone is feeling
as their light burns from a window,
and their hospital corridor sleeps
in the blue silence past midnight.
There are no traces, only reminders,
of the mother who grieves a child
after the bodies are pulled free
from the dusty bombed ruins,
and the child's face is a ghost.
Here are only rumours of happiness
hanging around the end of lines,
looking for something tangible
to which they might attach themselves,
the way the perfume of a lover
hovers over the scattered sheets
that have cooled and left the shape
of something that was once so real,
an island whose profile appears
as a sleeping body on the horizon
that wants to be named and touched
and holds out its arms to embrace you
as you walk through the spirit
of someone who once loved you,
a penny that had its luck run out
though you continue to value its worth.

The Man in the Street

When he wrote the secrets of the stars
on the garden wall of the rich man's club,
I stopped and asked him if mathematics
could be understood by the man in the street,
assuming that I was speaking of someone else.

And believing what he wrote was gibberish,
the patrons of the club had the bricks reversed,
but I know what lies on the other side,

and the way the inconsolable mathematician,
lacking clothes — his beard tangled with theorems —
froze to death one February night as stars
looked on in silence not wanting to get involved.

Mugs

The college mug, its logo faded
the way the faces of freshmen vanish
with old essays and failed tests;
the first love's mug that came with flowers
and a lollipop taped to the side;
one from the first job when being hired
told the world you'd become someone
and had the mug to prove it; the ones
that accumulated from conferences
and short vacations declaring how much
you loved a place you'll never see again;
appreciative sentimental mugs
about being a good parent, or the funky
earthenware hand-made good grips
that seemed like fine ideas at the time;
leftover milestone mugs from birthdays
with a date on it you can't retrieve;
they came into your life as benchmarks
against the rising flow of tea, coffee,
sympathy, and time until one by one,
as if meant to pass from sight
they are not there from simple wear of life;
when they are gone all you are left
is the taste of a Darjeeling before dawn,
or cocoa on a winter night as snow
falls outside your kitchen window
and you think of your life as all it held.

The Czar's Dog

There is a silent film of Alexis shot
as he plays with his spaniel, a stick
tugged between them, a moment's joy
in a brief life measured in dog years.
The animal chases the Prince frame right
to left. The film is over in ten seconds.

The Czar bends down. Courtier seconds
stand in the shadows, shadows shot
with jewelled sunlight. The moment is right
for happiness. They are playing with a stick,
the dog on hind legs. He leaps through years,
in the photograph inscribed simply "Joy."

The Winter Palace falls. The family and Joy
flee before the Bolsheviks, precious seconds
when a bone is buried, buried long years
of war and starvation, a mother lying shot
with a child in her arms. The old ways stick
to their paths; history cannot be set right.

The family lines up together. To their right
the spaniel crouches, his eyes full of joy
to be with them. He knows he must stick
by them wherever they go as the seconds
play keep away and a favourite ball is shot
skyward. Will it drop? Seems like years.

The basement. Seconds pass like years,
their backs against the striped wall, right
against the wall. They wait to be shot.
He is simply happy to be there. Their Joy.
He whimpers. The noises last just seconds
as they fall, falling like twigs, broken sticks,

and he shudders with a frightened cry, sticks
his nose in an executioner's hand. For years
those who knew the family asked if seconds
stretched like aeons as they died, and right
there, the dog knew the answer. Their Joy
lived long; freeze the film; you see a shot

of a boy with a stick, and right beside him his dog.
The years have not stolen that framed joy
of seconds shot in eternal happiness.

Anjou Pear

I am going to lie down in the afternoon light
and think of France,

imagine a girl in a smocked blouse,
her long black skirt trailing the meadow,

ask her what prize she offers
as an answer to her question —

what is more beautiful:

the sun vanishing at dusk on blossoms,
or dawn when a pear begins to ripen?

I have no answers but cannot forget
the taste of her sweet gift that trembles

as wind runs its fingers through an orchard
to touch the golden pear she brings.

The Doorframe from
Notre-Dame de Reugny

Part of the world's demise is not decay
but rearrangement, factual alterations
in a landscape, acquisitions that decry
entropy. The door is now in New York.
I run my hands over the stone columns
and smoothed joints, chisel channels
of those who knelt in the sun for angelus
and felt as if angels framed their work,
their eyes blind with the light of a door,
opened suddenly on daylight through which

larks passed on their way to vespers,
and the sparrows found evensong
in eaves and sang the holiness of stone,
because to make something beautiful
declares that there is no pain, no mortal
decay except that which is left behind
to argue the sad philosophy of time:
the mason dying in his wife's arms,
his children going off to war, perishing,
leaving behind their own marks on what

is made and remade until walls fall down.
Angels still pass this way. So do demons.
The craftsman knew that a door is more
than a door, a threshold is not a beginning
but the point at which a journey ends,
when the tools that transform the world
are set aside and there is another journey
standing straight ahead and beckoning.
Heaven knows there are more worlds
than this, and each one needs a door.

- Change -

Barber Shop

No lost love is an ordinary one;
no remembered death without its pity.
See how time can be undone
with words trimmed to simplicity.

No remembered death without its pity
could fill the passing of old places
with words trimmed to simplicity.
I remember the light in lost faces

could fill the passing of old places
to make me forget Saturday mornings.
I remember the light in lost faces,
men in a barber shop whose warnings

to make me forget Saturday mornings
became a future that happened inevitably —
men in a barber shop whose warnings
swept away as cuttings and debris

became a future that happened inevitably
pulling the survivors along, helpless,
swept away as cuttings and debris,
things no one saved from time and loss.

Pulling the survivors along, helpless
as hair wreaths cut from a bald head,
things no one saved from time and loss,
were cast down to the land of the dead.

As hair wreaths cut from a bald head,
cut me some slack from what is naught,
and cast down to the land of the dead
the souls of old men time forgot.

Cut me some slack from a bald head.
Remind me of the incense of aftershave,
the souls of old men time forgot
and the shining pates no barber could save.

Remind me of the incense of aftershave,
for no lost love is an ordinary one,
and the shining pates no barber could save
are purified by a Saturday morning sun.

The Thousand-Year Egg

What is buried may eventually rise:
the delicious life, lost treasures with black shells,
amber whites and pungent cheese-like yolks,

living proof that a sleeping beauty
lives after having slept so long.
The emperors of ancient China

believed in everlasting life,
that if buried with their household cast
they would rise and restart their reigns on cue.

In a dream of a winter morning a thousand years away,
my daughter wakes with half the day
consumed by teenage sleep.

She has probably grown in the night —
taller and more beautiful than yesterday,
and with her dishevelled hair,

red and radiant in the midday sun,
she passes before our kitchen window
translucent as amber when light shines through.

Rembrandt, Self-Portrait, 1660

We cannot always be what we wish to be,
cannot endure the weight of grace,
or possess forever the dreams we choose.
Look in his eyes. He is not staring at you.
He is fixed on the light from the gallery roof,
a light that falls but never rises,
the light of wisdom acquired in defeat —
for we cannot be what we wish to be,
or remain what we are when it has passed.

Everyone loves the depths of failure.
Such shadows make for nobility in art;
grey vapours over his right shoulder,
the peril of limits, and the turn of the mouth,
not in sadness but in sad awareness
that holding the world is to not hold on,
that to grow always means one must grow old,
and what is noble in age will grow more noble,
for to wish to be what one cannot be
is the one loving gesture permitted in art,
what crowds line up for on a summer's day
and travellers come to witness and test.

The black hat tilted toward the left
is the shadow he knew all souls must wear,
and his eyes, perplexed at what he knows to be true,
suggest your shadow will turn away,
the way the world turned away and love grew distant
until the canvas of his life went blank
and there was nothing else for him to portray.
To run out of characters in the theatre of the self
is the realization that the light is gone
and the paint will not speak when the sun returns;

but we are fortunate and the light still follows us
as we stare at those eyes that have long stared back,
for we are what we are and little else more
and to know that is wisdom
though of little respite.

The Passenger

The cruise company sent me a letter
describing how an elderly Florida woman

sailed the blue Caribbean until her death
when she no longer entertained horizons,

or tipped the toothy cruise director
for reminding her how to laugh.

She could endure the bad comedians,
cloying waiters, and fawning stewards,

could live through repeated rumba nights
and never forget the need to dance;

perhaps witness countless couples wed
while someone of a lesser rank kept watch,

and the regimen of lifeboat drills
were practice for when she'd disembark.

Every port, familiar as a second home,
each new buffet or napkin class

could welcome her as if brand new,
the way old places are reinvented

because they need to be some place else.
There is only so much planet to explore,

but the outline of an island dressed
for dawn in a rain forest mist,

or lightning over silhouetted mountains
as anonymous in the night as love,

were permanence enough for her.
Passengers climbed aboard

every time the circle closed,
yet voyaging with familiar strangers,

all of them so anxious to grow new,
became her way to say so long

while never admitting farewell.

The Birds

Among wild olive and strawberry trees,
And offering barley grains and wheat
We'll pray to them with outstretched hands
For all our wants.

— Aristophanes, *The Birds*

i

The sky could have been paved with song
before the sun went down in a golden city
with bright wings and a flight of fancy.

A lone gull above the evening in long
iambs of wings explores the outer edges
of his metropolis as a white wisp nudges

the sun into its after-dinner glow among
ornithology's catalogue. Birds woke me
today with their incessant broken screed

where each declared its place the wrong
place for others, and crapped on men below,
because birds are superior beings who

are descendants of love and night, and throng
with the higher orders. The gull screams
curses at earthlings and their puny dreams.

ii

The canary we kept caged for a dozen years
would sing its heart out, calling to cardinals
and jays at daybreak with sighs and signals

of a prisoner trying to raise alarms in ears
of the outside world. We planned a good burial
when it died, but something in its heart, a call

of unspoken freedom held it as it lay there
on the bottom of the cage, claws gripping a tall
invisible tree from where it could sing to us all.

iii

Wings are not necessarily blessings for a bird.
They create illusions, lead to boundaries,
point them south when a season varies,

leaving flight the only means of escape. The word
often comes on wings, but words define change,
know the pecking order of meaning, a frail range

of intonations, momentary exaggerations heard
in spilled passions or distractions; and what fails
always follows after them in plumed bright tails.

So they build utopian castles in the air, incur
the wrath of sleepers in the dawn, are watched
by those who love them, and as such are hatched

like great plans in the *commedia* of the absurd
where there is both suffering and soaring delight
as they go before us singing, to test the daylight.

iv

When I visited the city of winged desires,
the sun was ablaze, the air crazed
with wild song, and every note raised

a great hope of redemption that inspires
the soul to make sacrificial requests;
and there, among the birds, the nests

of golden thatch, eggs of hatchling choirs
rang out their vespers, the earth trembled,
and praise illumined the assembled.

Having passed through mortal fires,
I had anticipated less weighty
matters, but birds who are citizens of air,

have more on their minds — winged lyres
tuned to love, they know love is light
and light shines to make heaven brighter,

and grows brighter because the soul admires
virtue, feeds on it, and sings for love —
wake now. The birds are calling you to love.

The Unicorn Tapestries

for Mark Raynes Roberts

There are no such things as unicorns,
and though I saw one dancing once,
I was told to ignore extemporal beauty
and let it die with other great beliefs.

Moving through the woods one dawn
with just enough midsummer
to know of all the wonders of the heart,
I watched it drinking at a pristine pool.

Its blood was the purity of soft rain
that made allegories into gardens
and love into leaded windows
that let light inside a thought;

but men are as afraid of unicorns
as they are of poetry, for alicorns
are pens that write of passions;
what cannot be caged must be killed.

So when the unicorn was butchered,
and ladies watched it turn to salt,
I no longer heard the beauty of its hooves
or their rhythm on the heart like rain.

I let it die with other great beliefs.
I learned to ignore extemporal beauty.
I thought I saw one dancing once,
but there are no such things as unicorns.

Transmigration

Birds have wings
because in their souls
they believe they are
brothers to the sun.

When the sun sets
they cannot bear
to think of death
touching their wings

so they hide their faces
to imagine daylight.
They dream of worms.
They fly from fear.

No bird wants to die.
No bird wants to live
in dark treetops where
there are no other birds,

or where time waits
as if a songless silence,
stalking them with hunger
or just the pleasure to kill.

Something in birds says
begin again, go forth,
fly toward the rainbow
the way a raven searched

and a dove grew nervous,
returning with a twig,
as waters calmed
and a moon rose to chase the sun.

This is why birds follow
their shadows. This is why
they were given souls.
Look after them, they sing.

And if they lose themselves
they cannot find themselves.
They pull the sun into the day,
and summon morning to open your eyes.

– Entropy –

Miss Otis in The Cloisters

for Halli Villegas

In the clarity of brilliant daylight
with her eyes wide awake enough
to see through the white reflection
of love shining on ancient stone,
Miss Otis regrets she never cared
for the quietude of the Middle Ages
until this moment when a honey bee
hovered over a veil of lavender
and delicate roses bloomed matins
for the love of ideas in a garden.

A fountain slowly cools the holiness
the way pain is erased by libations,
though this is morning and the clarity
of a stone lion staring frankly ahead
has seen time's shadow in his roar,
and in all the beautiful summers passing
when hands were soft and the silence
of *basilico* was kind, and just, and true,
praise rang in the prayers between
whispered wings of swallows at angelus.

And suddenly Miss Otis turns and says
that time is only a whisper wandering
free of a book of hours and ripe time,
being neither hers to hold nor to give,
is something that can stand dead still
without feeling an ounce of old regret
or the need of an aspirin to remind her
of a moment's pure chivalric promise
that in the centre of an ancient garden

and among the splendor that is paradise
there is a peace that wants to listen
to the world's great soul, a grace note
in a poem to a woman whose forehead
is high and *makelesse* above her eyes,
because heaven is waiting to announce
that she is made of gold in sunlight,
and the world, or her handbag, is seated
on her lap, and she knows true beauty
as a queen knows the realm she holds.

The Harvest

The rounder, the heavier:
Spies, Cortlands, Wolf Rivers,
and Macs fell around us
like Empires and Snows,

and the sour perfume
of bruisers on the ground
grew vinegar pungent
as a sponge on the tongue.

Orchards are for faith
the way a frost says sleep
is for mourning in October
after a long, ripening day.

Time made apples to test
the soul of nature,
and what survives of it
says next year will be better,

while reaching up means
reaching higher for good ones,
ones always way too high,
and the pole on the picker

is always inches too short.
Its fingers became my hands,
and gently tugging to keep
the apple and not the node,

felt its soft surrender
when tired of the long fight
it came away as if lovers'
hands unclasping at dawn.

Jam

During canning season as each crop began,
my mother, grandmother, and the flavour
of summer fruit would fill the house
with song as they cut each piece into small
wedges for the stewing pot. My favourite
was *Blue Bells of Scotland* sung to peaches.

Imagine buttered toast and compote peaches
on a winter morning as a dark day began
with a veil of snow covering a favourite
face's smile, and the golden flavour
greeting me at breakfast. In delicate, small
ways, those women were the love in our house.

A crown-glass sealer jar could house
a mystery that kept our spirits up — peaches
that spread upon the tongue the way a small
taste of light illumines a room. So began
their ritual, inspecting every orb, fine flavour
perfuming their dripping hands, a favourite

one set aside to eat later with a favourite
cake or as a meal-time gift to house
another gesture of love. Picture them flavour
each rare moment when pectin in the peaches
jelled and the sweetness of the jam began
to set the way memory sets, and no charm too small

to be forgotten, no sadness, haunts the small
hours of the morning as they finished their favourite
and tightened the last jar. Every jam began
and ended in the same way — strawberries, a house
for seeds, inkling blueberries, ambrosial peaches —
each summer month a new fruit, a new flavour

before moving on to savories, the final flavour
tart as winter hardship. Nothing was too small
to be overlooked. Strawberries, blueberries, peaches —
the litany of our bounty, all leaving a favourite
moment of time in the quiet corners of our house
to remind us where we were and how we began;

and every story had its own flavour, a favourite
memory, an aroma, the small chronicles of a house
preserved like peaches from when time began.

Baconian Method

This is where a determined rumination
would be appropriate. A comment
on process. The process of commenting.
Phenomenon is all around. It is waiting
to be observed. Just now as you smiled —
was it something I said not worth
repeating? I want to say it again
so it might make your face light up
with the loveliness of irises in winter.
I will not push my luck. May I conclude
that repetition is madness if you
do not smile when I say it again?
Science and logic would say I'm wrong.
Would argue we fill a void with love
when there is nothing there to find.
Nothing that can be repeated. Only time
past. The memory of it. The deceit of hope.
Illumination of need. Fear of emptiness.
What is not repeated vanishes. What is
not tested may not stand the test of time.
I want to discover what gives you brilliance.
I want to form a law from it. Apply it
to all living things. To what we know,
and what we do. Know what is true now
will be true forever and always lasting.
I want to make a maxim of your light.
There is light in everything. Poets have
said so. They have spoken through time.
You are the breath that hangs in the air
after what you say on a winter morning.

I want my hands to hold that breath.
I want to hold the beauty of your life.
This world is probably a guess at best.
Let us guess the answer to this world.
Let us prove that love is ever constant.
Let us conclude love moves all things.

Origami Cranes

for Sadako Sasaki

i

To make a thousand origami cranes by hand,
to labour quietly over each fold and point

is to be granted one wish by the crane of cranes
the way wind is the wind of all good winds

even if it only touches one's hand.
Time could remake the world at any moment,

but instead it sets aside its arrow path
for a single moment of perfection.

When the cranes have disappeared, when flights
vanish from prairie coolies and summer rain,

one will wonder why the world had cranes,
and how their wings when spread upon the air

took flight to re-enact the spirit of creation,
and each one left its shadow on the clouds.

ii

To watch for miracles is like staring at the sun:
eventually one goes blind trying to see it all.

That is the nature of human wishes, a blindness
that arrives spread-winged on the air,

that balancing act on a single leg
or a rare appearance the Irish call luck.

Being touched by the unexpected is to be expected
but seldom realized.

Sadako Sasaki dreamed that cranes

would grant her the wish of the life she dreamed,
her body eaten by Hiroshima's blast, her eyes

staring at a god-light unleashed; she folded,
over six hundred origami cranes

                    to ask

for the right to ask one wish. One day an egret
stood at her window, and asked her to fly away.

iii

Be careful what you wish for, a teacher told me.
There is always a star that opens the night.

It is cold, and distant, and does not know me.
Inscrutable light, I trust you more than *senbazuru* birds.

Have wings to make life eternal. Have gentle breezes
to fly beyond time. Take my life as you would a dream,

and let it fly in the face of death. Show the world
a wish lasts forever, and forever is never beyond one's reach.

Crane of cranes and infinite wishes,
share my prayer with every sunrise.

iv

The day we were married the birds returned.
It was spring. Wings were endless blue above us.

We heard them chirping in the chapel's eaves,
heard them between the words of blessings

and tried to understand what they were saying.
Love and love's promises do things to the mind.

I wished I could respond to them, ask them favours.
Could you carry my prayers beyond their failures

to places where wishes are more than questions,
treated with the honour of poetic justice?

I have made enough cranes to make my prayers
come to our window and pronounce the word *yes*,

and I know they heard me. I still have you.
I want to make paper live a thousand years.

The Fall

Lying on the bedroom floor, he finds
hours become shadows of things beyond

the bed, chairs, and highboy.
The window mocks him. Through it

he sees the moon, the startled rabbit
running away having done its damage.

When they found him days later,
his hip a broken celery stalk,

there was little point in assigning blame.
He just had to fall a little farther

to reach the bottom of the darkness.
Rabbit, he wept, come back with my life.

Deer in the Headlights

That went away, this may also.

— Anglo-Saxon poem, *Deor*

Illusions and the salt lick of starlight
drive them from the mosquito brush
and reduce them to cleft-marks in dust,

burning Perseids that outlive their fall.
If I survived a collision with time
I would be asking the same questions

of frightened starlight in their eyes
as they emerge on the Government Road
to dissect the bark on summer cedars

in search of answers that do not exist.
They look with mythic disbelief
as the car swerves to save their legend,

and they dash — white tails flagging —
surrendering mercy and leaping for safety,
and my heart pounds as I imagine them.

Tonight, at dusk, on the farmhouse porch,
I thought of how we could have died.
Crickets cried for love in the ditches,

and phoebes mid-air ate their weight
as a fawnless doe stared from the orchard,
her eyes asking was there more to life?

Time amongst Quince

Time amongst sabled quince
is a troubadour's song
sung in countertenor to autumn air

where the sun gives alms
between branches, and meadow
and larks have departed,

leaving their high chantries
to the body of a warm afternoon,
though here there is still a gift,

a prize for knowing beauty
that is both power and diplomacy;
and though this tree is one of the last

of its kind gnarled by Ontario wind,
it is still standing from the day
someone had a dream-vision of an orchard

planted it in a question of eschatology,
while a serpent tempted himself
with the scent of paradise

and found better things to do
when the first fruit grew heavy enough
to make someone consider eternity.

NOTES TO THE POEMS

The title of this volume, *The Arrow of Time*, is a phrase used to explain the life of atomic particles by the British physicist, Arthur Eddington (1882–1944). In his treatise *The Nature of the Physical World*, Eddington coined the phrase "the arrow of time" to explain the relationship between matter and existence, suggesting that all things are moving through time but that they experience a series of phases until they break down: expansion, increase, cause, change, and entropy. I have used these phases as my section headings for the poems in this book.

"Young Rembrandt, 1637" is inspired by a self-portrait by the artist. It is part of the permanent collection of the Wallace Collection in London, England.

"Seven Magpies" is based on an old English augury rhyme that goes: "One for sorrow / Two for joy / Three for a girl, / Four for a boy. / Five for silver. / Six for gold, / And seven for a secret / Never to be told." Next to the GO Train platform at Bradford, on the edge of Holland Marsh north of Toronto, there is a field that is annually planted with green onions. When the train door opens for morning commuters, the smell of onions fills the car.

"Masterpieces": Wilson Bentley (1865–1931) was a Vermont farmer and photographer who set up a special studio in his barn for photographing snowflakes. He devised a system of capturing the flake on a black velvet background before it had a chance to melt. Over his career, he produced more than 110,000 images of various kinds of snowflakes. The collection is now in the Albright Knox Gallery in Buffalo, New York.

"Crystal Set": A crystal set is a radio that is able to receive radio signals without the benefit of a battery or electricity.

"Complications": A complication is a name for a function in a multi-function watch. Each complication expresses and measures some element of movements on Earth and in the stars. The largest number of complications known to have been built into a single time-piece is thirty-six in the Franck Mueller Aeternitas Mega 4, the world's most complicated wristwatch.

"Strawberries": Strawberries of the European genus *fragraria* became popular in Italy during the Roman period. The garden-variety straw-berry that we now eat — a mixture of the European variety and the North American wild strawberry — is larger though less sweet than the wild berry. A "dream-vision" poem is a medieval literary sub-genre where a character falls asleep, wakes in an allegorical world, and embarks on a quest to achieve a spiritual goal. An example of a "dream-vision" poem is *La Roman de la Rose* by Guillaume de Lorris and Jean de Meun (c. 1420–1430), where the dreamer attempts to obtain a kiss from a rose at the centre of a garden. The poem inspired the popular song "A Kiss from a Rose" by Seal.

"Turner's Spectacles": The British painter, J.M.W. Turner (1775–1851) spent a large part of his painting career staring into the sun to study the way levels of light transform the appearance of an object. The resulting damage to his eyes caused Turner to become severely presbyopic (near-sighted). When Turner died, his thick glasses, used for seeing objects up close, were retrieved from the artist's studio by the critic John Ruskin. They are now part of the collection in the Tate Britain Gallery in London. The reference to Babylon is a play on the old English children's rhyme, "How Many Miles to Babylon?" "How many miles to Babylon? / Three score and ten. / Can I get there by candle-light? / Yes and back again. / If your heels are nimble and light / You can get there by candlelight." There are some opinions that claim that the poem is a reference to Crusaders attempting to return to Scotland after meeting with failure abroad.

"Thirst": On his death bed, the Columbian novelist Gabriel Garcia Marquez called out for snow. On briefly regaining consciousness his last conversation was about how his father had taken him to see snow on the Andes as a young boy.

"Adam and Eve" is a painting by Lucas Cranach, completed c. 1500. It is now part of the permanent collection of the Courtauld Institute in London, England. The epigraph from Latin, "ut animata viderent Dominum natum" is part of the Church of England high mass that is sung, largely in Latin, on Christmas Eve. The statement means "God was born among the animals."

"Hans Memling's 'The Donne Triptych'": This painting from about 1478 is in the collection of the National Gallery, London, England. The "Donne" in the title bears no reference to the poet John Donne. It refers, instead, to the donor who paid for the triptych to be painted.

"The Preliminary" refers to a sketch an artist makes in the field (away from his studio) in preparation for a larger canvas. John Constable (1776–1837) did a small "preliminary" of his birthplace on the Stour River in East Bergholt, Suffolk, in 1802. The larger painting, intended to be completed in the studio, was never undertaken, though part of the study appears in other, better-known canvases. The canvas of the preliminary sketch in oils, known simply as "The White Horse, East Bergholt" was shown in the winter of 2014 at the Victoria and Albert Museum, London.

"The Mathematics of Sunflowers": The Fibonacci sequence, according to mathematicians and botanists, is the numerical sequence for a vortex in vegetative life. The sequence is 1, 1, 2, 3, 5, 8, 13, 21, 34, 55, 89, 144, etc. It is the mathematical structure of a spiral emanating from a single centre point. It can been seen in the seed-bed face of a sunflower.

"Nanking": The city of Nanking was bombed and the population butchered by the Japanese Imperial Army in an event known as the "Rape of Nanking" on December 13, 1937. The "Hundred Boys" is both a Chinese folk tale and a tapestry and drapery pattern popular among European and North American missionaries at the beginning of the twentieth century.

"The Thin Man": My father's Kodak movie camera was a wind-up camera that operated without the use of battery power. One could make time speed up by allowing the camera to wind down as it recorded a scene.

"The Czar's Dog" involves a true story about an English springer spaniel named Joy that was given as a gift by George V and ·Queen Mary to Czar Nicholas II and his family. The dog was the only survivor of the immediate Russian royal family who were massacred at Ekaterinburg. Joy was eventually found by a White Russian (Czarist) officer who brought the dog with him across Asia after the collapse of Czarist forces. The officer returned the dog to England and gave it to King George V. Joy is buried in the grounds of Windsor Castle.

"Anjou Pear": The "question" that is being asked references the question posed to Prince Paris of Troy when he was asked by the three goddesses, Athena, Aphrodite, and Hera, who among them was the most beautiful. When Paris answered badly and chose Aphrodite, his failure to answer "correctly" was one of the causes of the Trojan War. The event appears in art as "The Judgement of Paris." The prize that was offered for guessing correctly was, some say, a golden apple or possibly a quince, but more likely a pear.

"The Doorframe at Notre-Dame de Reugny": This doorframe was salvaged in 1923 from the ruins of a small French country church. It is now part of the permanent collection known as "The Cloisters" in New York's Metropolitan Museum of Art. (See also "Miss Otis in The Cloisters.")

"Rembrandt, Self-Portrait, 1660": This painting is part of the permanent collection of the Metropolitan Museum of Art in New York City.

"The Passenger": In January 2015, I received a letter from a local travel agency that recounted the story of a Florida woman who lived out her life aboard a cruise ship after the death of her husband. The letter was an attempt to entice me to buy a cruise.

"The Birds": The playwright Aristophanes claimed that birds had built a utopian city in the sky, and that high-flying birds such as seagulls went there often to escape the problems generated by mankind.

"Transmigration" is the process whereby a soul is reborn into a different form after death. The final lines of the poem are from the Gospel of Matthew: "If I save myself, I lose myself. If I lose myself, I save myself." This passage is also used by Alfred, Lord Tennyson, in "The Grail," part of the *Idylls of the King*, where it is inscribed on the chair in which only the one true knight may sit.

"The Harvest": Newer varieties of apples have replaced some of the older ones in the orchards of southern Ontario in recent years. The older varieties include the Red Delicious, often simply called Delicious, and known as a hard, tart, baking apple. Empires are still readily available, but among the vanishing varieties is a large, sweet baking apple called Wolf River. People used to say of it: "one apple, one pie." There is also the Snow, which is dark red on the outside and pale pink inside, grown as a sweet eating apple.

"The Unicorn Tapestries": These are part of the permanent collection of The Cloisters portion of the Metropolitan Museum of Art in New York City. They depict the capture, penning, death and beheading of a unicorn. An alicorn is the anatomical term for a narwhal tusk or a unicorn's horn.

"Baconian Method": This method of investigation was devised by the natural philosopher, essayist and political thinker, Sir Francis Bacon (1561–1626), for testing and proving observations in the physical world through a process of inductive reasoning. Modern science is a product of the Baconian method.

"Origami Cranes": Sadako Sasaki was a young woman who suffered severe burns and radiation poisoning as a result of the atomic bomb dropped on Hiroshima. In Japanese folk traditions, it is believed that a person who can make one thousand origami cranes will be granted their wish. Sasaki died in 1955 before her wish could be granted. *Senbazuru* is the Japanese name given to one thousand paper origami cranes held together by strings.

ACKNOWLEDGEMENTS

"Seven Magpies" appeared in *Acta Victoriana*.

"The Fall" appeared in the *Hart House Review*.

"Explaining Romanticism to My Daughter," "Deer in the Head-lights," "A Book of Things," "The Mathematics of Sunflowers" and "Nanking" were finalist poems in the Gwendolyn MacEwen Poetry Prize and appeared in *Exile Literary Quarterly*.

"The Harvest" appeared on the blog *Sunday Crush*.

"The Thin Man" appeared in *FreeFall* and won third place in their annual poetry competition.

My sincerest thanks to Ronald Hatch of Ronsdale Press for his brilliant feedback and for his encouragement and perseverance to help me find the best words in the best order; to the staff and designers at Ronsdale Press for all the fine work they do; to Karen Wetmore and the staff of Grenville Printing at Georgian College for the care they brought to the evolution of this project; to the staff at the Courtauld Institute in London, England, for permitting me to spend hours seated in study in front of various paintings that inspired some of these poems; to the staff of The Cloisters of the Metropolitan Museum of Art in New York for their kindness and patience; to Adam Zachary for reading these poems in progress and offering his constructive and creative feedback; to Halli ("Miss Otis") Villegas and David Bigham for taking me to New York where these poems began; to Dr. Carolyn Meyer for pointing out details I might have otherwise missed; and to my mother who took the family to London where these poems found their final form. Thank you to my daughter Katie, and to my wife Kerry for their inspiration, thoughtful words, and for listening.

ABOUT THE AUTHOR

Bruce Meyer is the author of more than forty-five books of poetry, short fiction, nonfiction, literary journalism, and textbooks. His broadcasts, such as *The Great Books* and *Great Poetry: Poetry is Life and Vice-Versa* with Michael Enright, are among the CBC's bestselling spoken-word audio cds. His most recent books include the anthology *We Wasn't Pals: Canadian Poetry and Prose of the First World War* (co-edited with Barry Callaghan with an afterword by Margaret Atwood), the poetry collections *The Obsession Book of Timbuktu, Testing the Elements* and *The Seasons,* as well as the short story collection *A Chronicle of Magpies.* He is professor of English at Georgian College in Barrie, Ontario, and visiting professor of literature at Victoria College in the University of Toronto. He was the inaugural poet laureate of the City of Barrie from 2010 to 2014. He lives in Barrie with his wife and daughter.